A MUSIC BOOK SERVICES PAPERBACK

This is a Carlton Book
Exclusively distributed in the U.S.A. by MBS Corporation,
16295 N.W. 13th Ave., Ste. B, Miami, Florida 33169

Text and design © 1995 Carlton Books Limited
CD Guide format © 1995 Carlton Books Limited

ISBN 1 886894 24 8

Printed in Italy

THE AUTHOR
Jon Ewing is a freelance writer and proprietor of Vigilante
Publications. He will do anything legal for cash or anything illegal just
for fun. This is his fourth book.

The author would like to thank: Green Day, Rob Cavallo, Jim Baltutis at
WEA West Coast, Wags at WEA East Coast, Lawrence Acres at WEA
U.K. and Simon R. Barry.

Picture Acknowledgments
The publishers would like to thank the following sources for their kind
permission to reproduce the pictures in this book:
London Features; Pictorial Press; Redferns;
Retna Pictures; Rex Features; S.I.N.

Every effort has been made to acknowledge correctly and contact the
source and/or copyright holder of each picture, and Carlton Books
Limited apologises for any unintentional errors or omissions which will
be corrected in future editions of this book.

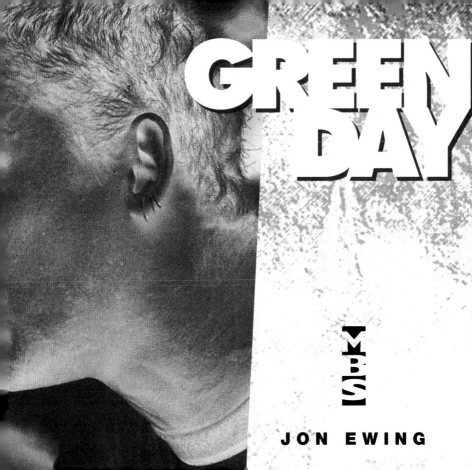

GREEN DAY

JON EWING

Contents

INTRODUCTION 6

1972-1991 10

1991-1993 36

1993-1994 54

1994 68

THE PRESENT AND FUTURE 100

DISCOGRAPHY 116

CHRONOLOGY 117

INDEX 119

Introduction

They have only come because everyone told them not to. They arrive from Albany by stretch limousine and helicopter, straight into the most expensive and technically complex rock music event of all time. Out in front of the South Stage at Woodstock, the audience of 300,000 are chanting "Green Day! Green Day!"

The trio take to the stage. There's the geekish lead singer, hair dyed shocking blue, his battered guitar smothered with stickers. There's the green-haired drummer, dressed in baggy, unwashed beach punk T-shirt and short pants. And there's the lean, clean bass player, looking somehow out of place until he leaps recklessly into the air for the band's opening number, 'Welcome To Paradise.'

It's 1994. A year in which America is celebrating Ace Ventura and Forrest Gump as heroes; and it's the year in which Green Day have skewered the rock world with a few well-timed reminders of punk rock vitality. They're dumb, they're unpredictable—straight from the animal house, with dookie for brains.

Down below the stage, the crowd is working itself into a frenzy. The security team is grabbing at flailing arms and

"Looks like dookie from here..."—Mike Dirnt about to lose his front teeth at Woodstock II.

Dookie heroes: Left-right, Billie Joe
Armstrong, Tre Cool, Mike Dirnt.

legs, pushing them back into the
heaving mass of bodies as the audience
seems determined to take over the
show. Pretty soon, lumps of mud from
the Saugerties arena are splattering on
to the stage. "We suggest that you
throw mud," deadpans Billie Joe
Armstrong. "That's fun."

The crowd needs no further
encouragement. Billie Joe races the
band through a set of high-octane punk
pop—'One Of My Lies', 'Chump',
'Longview', 'Basket Case'—and the
mud packs keep coming, raining down
around the tattooed trio as they goon
around the stage. As the melodic
'Paper Lanterns' dissolves into a riot of
noise, the stage, and everyone on it, is
sticky with dirt. Billie gently puts down

his favorite guitar and begins pelting
missiles back into the moshpit. Both he
and the crowd are in heaven. The
security team and pay-per-view
cameramen, cowering under big sheets
of clear plastic, don't seem so sure.

Pretty soon, the music has given
way to a display of bug-eyed clowning
as Billie Joe drops his Sta-Prest pants
and does mud-covered star jumps in
front of a worldwide television
audience. A fan climbs on the stage to
give bass player Mike Dirnt an ecstatic
embrace, at which an over-enthusiastic
security man bundles into them both,
sprawling on the floor and knocking
out Mike's front teeth into the bargain.

The music stops. It's all over. Green
Day have turned the world's most
state-of-the-art concert into a messy,
juvenile, ludicrous joke. Billie Joe's face
is beaming. His work here is done.

1972-1991

"**M**y dad was a jazz drummer. He would go to bars, play, smoke pot with his friends—what people in jazz do. I never really knew him too well. And my mom was into country music, she always listened to Hank Williams," says Billie Joe who was born William Armstrong on February 17, 1972. "I don't think they disliked rock—they were really into music in general. I have a lot of older siblings; I've got a brother who's old enough to be my father. And he's listened to a lot of stuff from Guess Who to the Who. And my mom was kind of an Elvis freak, so the first album I ever bought was Elvis Presley's *The Sun Sessions*."

Billie Joe Armstrong was the youngest and wildest of six children. "Mom gradually got less strict with each kid," Billie confesses. A musical prodigy, he got his first experience of performing at five when he was dragged out to hospices and homes to sing for the patients. His father was a truck driver and sometime jazz

Billie Joe Armstrong, guitar/vox: "I couldn't care less if people think I'm insignificant because I'm 22 years old. That's great. We caused a generation gap. Great. Most of the bands around now, I've been playing music longer than they have, and I'm also way younger than they are."

1972-1991

In their early teens, Billie Joe and Mike learned to play Van Halen's 'Ain't Talking About Love'. The duo eventually lost interest in heavy metal, but their love of gymnastics will never die.

musician, who tragically died of cancer when Billie was only ten years old. His last and most significant gift to the boy was an electric guitar. The instrument struck no chords with Billie Joe's teachers, who never recognized his gift for music and gave him no real guitar training. "I still can't read music and I only know about three chords," he says now. "But that's all you need."

"Our family changed a lot because my parents had been very kid-oriented," says Anna Armstrong, Billie Joe's sister. "And all of a sudden my mother withdrew and threw herself into waitressing. The family structure broke up. Then my mother remarried about a year or two afterward, and that was a big change for the negative. I'd say we were as dysfunctional as any family with the death of a father, a stepfather who no one liked and almost losing our mother at the same time. We were a very physical family. There was a lot of fighting among the siblings, a lot of hitting. I don't know where that anger came from."

RODEO, CA
Apart from the huge refinery which provides jobs for most of its inhabitants, Rodeo, CA's most famous landmark is a Safeway supermarket. It's a community of tract homes on the far edge of San Francisco's East Bay. In the words

of *Rolling Stone*'s Chris Mundy, it's "the kind of town that thankfully flashes by in the time it takes to change the radio station." Not surprisingly, Billie Joe's first taste of rock music came not from his school friends, but from a couple of new kids on the block. Every weekend, two brothers called Matt and Eric would visit their dad who lived just up the street from Billie's house in Rodeo. "They would bring all these new tapes with them," he recalls, "I remember listening to 'Too Fast For Love' by Motley Crüe a lot when I was 11 or 12. Then they started getting heavily into punk rock—they brought out DOA records, and TSOL, and the Dead Kennedys, stuff like that. Then they started riding skateboards, and I was like 'Wow, these guys are cool.'"

HEAVY METAL MADNESS

Mike Dirnt was actually born Michael Pritchard on May 4, 1972. His natural mother was a heroin addict who gave him up for adoption. The couple who took him were a native American woman and her white husband, but their irreconcilable differences led them to split up when Mike was only seven.

At first he lived with his father, later with his mother. It was a tough childhood—tough enough that his

> "The beauty of the punk thing is that everyone has their own interpretation— like the Bible."
>
> *BILLIE*

elder sister left home when she was just 13. "There were all sorts of things happening," says Mike. "When I was in fourth or fifth grade, my mom stayed out all night, came home the next day with a guy, and he moved in. I'd never met the guy before, and all of a sudden he's my stepdad.

"We didn't get along for years. Later on, when I hit high school, my mom moved away from us, and me and my stepdad got real close. He instilled a lot in me. But then he died when I was 17. The one thing my family did give me is blue-collar morals."

When he was ten, Mike met Billie Joe Armstrong in their school cafeteria one day in 1982. A friendship that has lasted a lifetime blossomed from a mutual desire to play heavy metal guitar.

"If you wanted to hear music in our town, you had to play it," said Mike in *Rip* magazine. "We didn't have a record store in town. We were little kids, and we had no way to get money—our parents were counting every dime, you know—but we saved up ourselves and Billie Joe got a guitar and played stuff. Then I started savin' like crazy. It took me a while, but I learned to play guitar, and then I finally got one… it was the funniest thing we ever could do. Me and Billie Joe jammed, together and with other people. We tried different bands and we played in, like, talent shows and stuff at the school."

In the duo's early repertoire were such gilt-edged classics as 'Ain't Talking About Love' by Van Halen and Def Leppard's 'Photograph'. At first they played only cover versions of dumb rock anthems, but Billie eventually

> ## "Then all of a sudden we got introduced to punk music and it was the coolest fuckin' thing."
>
> *MIKE*

got bored of playing along to records and decided to write his own songs. On reaching the maturity of the eighth grade, Mike and Billy vowed that they should now play only original material—with the odd exception.

SWEET CHILDREN

When they were both in high school, Mike got a bass and left the guitar in Billie's capable hands. Using the name Sweet Children, Mike and Billie played their first gig together in the

lounge of Rod's Hickory Pit, a roadside cafe in Vallejo where Billie's mom was working. They were 15 years old. After that they played anywhere they could, although seldom with any money changing hands. Once, a gig was interrupted by a telephone call from Billie Joe's mother who insisted that he come home to finish his chores.

Their first record appeared in 1987. The *Sweet Children* EP, released on the Skene label, was sold primarily by the band at their own gigs. Featuring a barrage of noise and unintelligible lyrics, the eponymous title track lacked the

Mike Dirnt, bass/vox: "We grew up in Berkeley, which is the fuckin' methamphetamine capital of California, so everything was irrelevant to us."

The Replacements and Hüsker Dü (following page) were the darlings of mid-Eighties college radio, an influence very apparent in Green Day's recordings.

infectious melody of Billie's later material, although the opening bars are a dead ringer for forthcoming classic 'Welcome To Paradise'. The EP featured a raucous cover of the Who's 'My Generation', a fave band of Billie Joe's who long ago might have been close in spirit to Green Day. Billie Joe has often admitted, "I sound like an Englishman impersonating an American impersonating an Englishman," and it was as true then as it is today. As a matter of historical interest, the EP can now be heard on the *Kerplunk!* CD.

Around this time, Mike's mother decided to move out of town to Santa

> "He loves English music. Probably most of his favorite bands are English: Beatles, Sex Pistols, Clash, Who..."
>
> ROB CAVALLO ON BILLIE

Rosa, about 50 miles away. Instead of going with her, Mike asked Billie's mother if he could rent the room on the side of their house. She agreed, so Mike got a job as a cook to pay the rent—about $250 a month. But at night, he and Billie would play...

"Then all of a sudden we got introduced to punk music and it was the coolest fuckin' thing," recalls Mike. "I mean, here we are playing loud music on shitty amps and everything and that's exactly what they were doing. It wasn't so much how they influenced us, it just kept us energized."

It was at this time that they began using the phrase "green day." It comes from an offhand remark by that celebrated linguistic icon Ernie, of the educational children's TV show *Sesame Street*. For Billie Joe and Mike it became an in-joke, a personal slang. A green day is one of those long, lackadaisical days viewed through a pall of smoke, the kind of day when nothing gets done and one hour just slips nonchalantly into another.

The surreal "Why does one and one make two?" lyrics of 'Green Day' painted a perfect picture of the ticklish, dizzy feeling of

intoxication. Billie Joe had written the song after an early experience of smoking pot—it's "basically about staring up at the ceiling thinking about a girl and being stoned," he says. 'Green Day' seemed to sum up Billie and Mike's unique attitude, and somehow the name stuck. Ironically, Green Day has become the least appropriate name imaginable for one of the hardest-working bands in the business. Green days are few and far between when you are on the road.

LOOKOUT!

In their sophomore year, Mike and Billie Joe left Rodeo and the Armstrong home and moved into a squat in West Oakland—a move which was to become the inspiration for 'Welcome To Paradise'. Mike and Billie Joe were jamming with other bands, individually and together, and even played a few gigs with local covers bands. Mike joined up with the Crummy Musicians as a vocalist, and Billie played guitar with the Corrupted Morals. But despite these distractions, they began to take Green Day very seriously. They hooked up with a drummer called John Kiffmeyer and decided to go after a record contract. There was only one obvious choice— Berkeley's foremost punk label, Lookout!

At first, Lookout! president Lawrence Livermore was unimpressed. He hoped to put the trio off by insisting that they make the 200-mile trip north to Mendocino county to audition for him in a little shack. Luckily for him, the band agreed to his terms. However, when they arrived, the owner was nowhere to be found

> "I've felt for as long as I've known them that they had the capacity to be one of the biggest bands of our time."
>
> *LARRY LIVERMORE*

and they were left standing outside the gates in the rain. In order to take shelter they broke in, quickly coming to the conclusion that there was no roof. To add insult to injury, the electricity supply had been cut off. However, where other bands would have admitted defeat, Green Day were implacable. With Livermore's help they rigged up a generator and played for an audience of 12 kids, each holding a candle. Livermore was very pleasantly surprised.

"I first saw them when they were 16," remembers Larry Livermore—although logic dictates they were more like 17 the night of the fateful gig in 1989. "And I thought Beatles... they had that early-Sixties, British Invasion kind of energy. It was just really bright and sparkly... I've felt for as long as I've known them that they had the capacity to be one of the biggest bands of our time. People laughed at me. Some people will probably still laugh at me, but they're laughing a lot less now." Livermore was so impressed that he put up the $600 or so for two days of recording to release their first album, *39/Smooth*.

SLAPPY DAYS

Even now, a number of tracks stand out as gems on *39/Smooth*. The opening 'At The Library' has the infectious guitar riff and beat-skipping rhythm that has become a Green Day trademark, along with Billie's unrequited, love-sick lyrics in a song about a very reluctant pick-up artist. John Kiftmeyer's only contribution, 'I Was There', is lyrically more sentimental than Billie Joe's material, but the harmonies of the chorus are the most irresistible on the record. The chugging guitar sound of 'Disappearing Boy' is the pure essence on which all Green Day's material is based, while '16' cuts straight to the teen-angst quick, desperately panicking as youth slips away. 'Rest' is the token slow track—its spiralling guitar sound so beautiful you wish they would play slow songs more often. As a follow up, 'The Judge's Daughter' spreads the

band's wings further still with a dash of Long Ryders-style folk punk.

Three of the four tracks from their sparkling first single, the *Slappy EP* (now available on the *1,039/Smoothed Out Slappy Hours* CD) were inspired by Billie's first love affair with a girl called Jennifer. The brilliantly catchy 'Paper Lanterns' features the words: "I'm understanding now that / We are only friends / To this day I'm asking why / I still think about you"—a sentiment directed toward a lost love, as Billie explains. "She's the one that got away. She's a couple of years older than I am. You know, a 16-year-old guy wanting to be in love with some girl. It wasn't quite there as

Tre Cool, drums/vox: "We don't like superstars and rock idols."

far as she was concerned, but I was there." The fourth track was a splendid cover version of Berkeley band Operation Ivy's 'Knowledge', which still appears in Green Day set lists today. Also available on the CD is the second, rather less inspiring four-song *1,000 Hours* EP.

SCHOOL DAZE

This sudden interest in their music put new pressures on Billie Joe and Mike, who were still at school. "Everybody I've ever known in any position of authority was tellin' me 'Dude, your band's failing—you need to go to fuckin' college'," Mike once recalled. "They never stopped.

Posing with their own customized Phoenix library bus, as driven by Frank Wright, Snr.

27

> "I couldn't care less if people think I'm insignificant because I'm 22 years old. That's great. We caused a generation gap. Great. Most of the bands around now, I've been playing music longer than they have, and I'm also way younger than they are."
>
> *BILLIE*

They never listened."

"Adrienne asked me what I'll do when our kid wants to drop out of school," Billie Joe told journalist Alex Foege in LA, early in 1995. "But what can you do? You can't change their mind. You can try to talk them out of it, but at the same time I know how evil school is. I fucking spent the worst years of my life in high school. It held me back from doing what I wanted to do. Nothing in it was interesting.

Opinions are force-fed to you. You're forced to read—which is evil. You can't force someone to read. That's no way of dealing with people in society. 'Do this, or suffer the consequences.'

"I write a lot about being a loser because I was conditioned to think that way. I was brainwashed to think that I was nothing compared to these people, these so-called geniuses who were teaching me all that crap. So I was like 'OK, that'll be my art form:

being a fucking idiot, being a loser.' If that's what I was trained to think I am, then that's what I'm going to do, and I'm going to do it the best way I possibly can. Now I'm 'losing' in a big way."

Billie Joe dropped out of high school on February 16, 1990, one day before his 18th birthday, midway through his senior year and seven days before the debut Green Day album arrived in record stores. He had decided long ago to concentrate on writing and playing—school had become nothing but a mild distraction. "When I was going to drop out of high school," Billie says, "I gave one teacher my drop-out slip. He just looked at me and said 'Who are you?'"

Billie Joe was encouraged to drop out by his mother, who never graduated herself. "I still have nightmares about being behind in class," confides Billie today. "I'll have these dreams where I'm getting an 'incomplete' in class." However, at the time he had bigger and better dreams—he was already beginning to conceive the batch of songs which would become Green Day's second album, *Kerplunk!*.

THE FIRST TOUR

Mike found it tough to cope with studying and working, especially when his mother wasn't around to authorize his work-related absentee slips and term reports. Two unexcused absences lost him a full grade point and at the end of the senior year he was down to C's, D's and F's instead of the A's and B's he had worked hard to achieve. "I took my mom aside," he recalls. "I said 'This is how it is. You have so much shit going on in your life, so if once every semester you ask me if I've done my homework and jump all over my case, that's not right. Have I failed yet? No. And I'm going to graduate if you stay off my back. The one time in your life you choose to have morals, and it's going to fuck me up. Don't play mom once a year. It doesn't fucking cut it.'"

While John Kiffmeyer and Mike continued at school, Billie Joe concentrated on booking a summer 1990 tour for the band, and the day after Mike's graduation from Pinole Valley they set off together to play 45 dates across the country. However, the tour was too much for John, who had ambitions to go to college. Mike later went on to take more than a year's worth of courses at a community college. Billie Joe did not.

He just wanted to keep the band together. As a temporary measure, former Sweet Child Al Sobrante was drafted in on drums (Sobrante was later credited as Executive Producer for his work on *Kerplunk!* arrangements). However, Billie Joe and Mike were in search of a permanent drummer. They didn't have to look far to find one.

THE MAKING OF COOL

New guy Edwin Frank Wright III, born December 9, 1972, grew up in Willits, in the remote, picturesque redwood country of Northern California. His father was a former Vietnam War

"We've made a lot of people feel good about the fact that they're lonely, loser geeks," boasts Billie. "Ugly, fat, skinny, anything."

30

helicopter pilot working as a truck driver who had retreated to the hippie ambience of the Mendocino mountains to escape the rat race.

At the age of 12 Frank, as he was usually known, stumbled across his nearest neighbor—about a mile away from home—the 30-year-old punk vocalist Lawrence Livermore.

When Livermore's band the Lookouts was in need of a drummer, the singer invited his pubescent neighbor to join the band, rechristening him Tre Cool. "They wouldn't even let me have cymbals for a long time," gripes Tre. "Lawrence locked them up, and after a while he would take them out one at a time and let me use them." From then on, Tre passed the time by playing with the Lookouts and jamming with local jazz musicians.

> "All you do is get fucked up. There's nothing to do. It's like 'What'd you do yesterday?'—'Smoked a fatty and drank a six pack.' You smoke a fatty and drink a six pack. You just sit there and rot."
>
> *TRE COOL ON HIS HOMETOWN*

When the Lookouts recorded their album, the first release on Lookout! Records in 1986, 12-year-old Tre was there behind the drum kit.

When he reached his sophomore year, at high school in Mendocino, Tre Cool was class president. But he was undernourished by the parochial, outmoded school system. So, he sat and passed a graduate equivalency exam. He sought inspiration partly from the local community college but mostly from music.

The first release on Larry Livermore's influential Berkeley-based label, which would become the home of Green Day as well as fellow Gilman Street residents Operation Ivy and the Mr T Experience, was *One Planet One People*. Recorded in October 1986, it blasted out 22 tracks in just under half-an-hour (the longest track being less than two-and-a-half minutes) and features Larry Livermore on guitar and vocals, Tre Cool on drums and vocals, and the mysteriously-named Kain Kong on bass.

The sound was fast and uncompromising, delivering Livermore's vision of Political Correctness and the dysfunctionalization of American youth from the days when Reagan was in the saddle. Songs like 'Fourth Reich', 'Nazi Amerika', 'Nazi Dreams' and 'Don't Cry For Nicaragua' shared a kinship with the Dead Kennedys, sizzling with real venom. Covers of the Rolling Stones' 'Last Time' and Bob Dylan's 'Baby Blue' were tossed into the firing line and blasted by the Lookouts' patented speed folk.

Tre added his own contribution to the polemic with his lyrics to the scathing 'The Mushroom Is Exploding': "All the government is achieving is a one-way ticket to hell."

Billie Joe joined the fray years later, adding guitar to the Lookouts'

> "I lost the scene where I came from. Not necessarily friends—I know who my friends are, who I'm going to be hanging out with for the rest of my life. I've lost the feeling of a community. Not just in terms of music but arts and 'zine writers, too. A lot of people can't get our older music because there were a lot of inside jokes involved in the music and the lyrics."
>
> *BILLIE*

cut 'Kick Me In The Head' on the Lookout! label's double LP *A Can Of Pork* in 1992. The set also featured 'North Berkeley' by Downfall, a band comprised of ex-Operation Ivy members Matt Freeman, Lint Armstrong and Dave Mellow, who lasted only four months together before breaking up—Matt and Lint went on to form current Epitaph Records faves, Rancid.

THE BERKELEY SCENE

924 Gilman Street is not much to look at. Situated just off I-80, it's an old garage building backing on to a wicker shop in a run down industrial area of northwest Berkeley. However,

since the late-Eighties, this club has been the center of the Berkeley underground music scene. It was the place to go to see all of the East Bay's finest punk bands—the Lookouts, Operation Ivy, Neurosis, and of course Green Day.

The beauty of Gilman Street is that it is inclusive—anyone can join the club if they can raise the buck membership fee. They don't serve alcohol, but they do serve coffee, sodas and candy—and the prices are low because Gilman Street is a non-profit making club run by volunteers. They're in it for the music, but they invite all comers. Membership meetings are regularly scheduled every first and third Saturday of the month at 5pm and bookings are made democratically by the members' Alternative Music Foundation committee.

To Billie and Mike, Gilman was a very special part of their lives. "We've played to 20,000, 30,000 people," says Billie Joe, "and I still haven't felt the same thing that I felt playing that place." For Tre Cool, the feeling was equally magnificent. He describes Gilman Street as a "punk rock Mecca"—a spiritual heartland.

Tre had known Green Day for some time as part of the tight-knit Gilman Street scene—he had even helped out John Kiftmeyer with drum tuition. So, when recording for *Kerplunk!* began in May 1991 and Green Day were without a drummer, Billie and Mike signed up Tre Cool. Green Day, as we know the band today, was born.

1991-1993

"Some of the old stuff really shreds," boasts Mike today. "I mean, any of those albums could have done just as good on Warners, but when you're recording on punk budgets—$600 was our budget for the first album—you can't use a very high-budget studio, so it's not as listener-friendly."

Green Day's second album, *Kerplunk!*, was recorded in May and September 1991. In Britain, *New Musical Express* critic Simon Williams quickly spotted their commercial leanings, pronouncing the band to be a "storming-but-soothing antidotal cream to smear on the current rash of grunge merchants."

Kerplunk! has an exquisitely spontaneous feel even today, partly because of the primitive production values but also because a few of the tracks (including '80', 'Welcome To Paradise', 'No One Knows' and 'One Of My Lies') were brand new, written only a week or two before the recording.

Rhyming "some call it nice" with "welcome to paradise" may be one of Billie Joe's all-time worst couplets, but nothing can detract from the potency of this dynamic, coming-of-age song.

As a teenager, Billie earned the nickname Two Dollar Bill by selling joints for a couple of bucks apiece.

"It's like 'Everything sucks but we're having fun anyway.'" says Tre. "It's a 'fuck you' sort of negativity, because we'll look you in the eye and still smile, even if horrible things are happening to you." A chorus bristling with juvenile pride and suburban bile is brilliantly balanced with an instrumental break which builds from a sleepy bass riff into a crashing crescendo of pogo power. It was one of Green Day's greatest moments to date, but there was more to this album than 'Paradise' alone.

'Christie Road' is the slow track, another restrained ballad to an industrial hometown which ups the tempo toward a vigorous conclusion. 'Dominated Love Slave' is a country and western novelty song which still gets funnier every time you hear it, while '80' betrayed Billie Joe's

37

maturing ear for melody with a classic Green Day theme of being driven insane by a long-distance love affair. "He makes a plan to take a stand / But always ends up sitting," sings Billie in an ode to JD Salinger's confused hero of *The Catcher In The Rye*, 'Who Wrote Holden Caulfield?', predating Nirvana by 12 months by coining the slacker motto "Oh well, never mind". The album comes to a conclusion with the distinctive twang of an acoustic guitar, giving way to the Monkees-style pop swell of 'Words I Might Have Ate'—a perfectly bitter-sweet climax.

Green Day's choice of live cover versions is diverse to say the least. Favorites include Joni Mitchell's 'Big Yellow Taxi', Survivor's 'Eye Of The Tiger', 'C Yo Yus' by Fifteen and, of course, the classic 'Knowledge' by Operation Ivy.

> "We used to go out and print merchandise over our guitar cases."
>
> *MIKE*

ON THE ROAD

With the release of the new album, Green Day's popularity was growing nationwide. Already Lookout!'s most popular signing to date, requests for live appearances were coming in every day. Between 1990 and 1993 they toured on average for seven months of the year.

Early days on the road were far from easy, but they were always eventful. Their first trip to Canada was in a compact car so small they had to sit with their instruments on their laps all the way. They played in towns as distant and remote as Billings, Montana and Rapid City, South Dakota. At times they had to beg for quarters at gas stations to make it to the next gig. On one memorable occasion, they arrived at a venue to find that the promoters had canceled and split; but, instead of turning around, they hastily arranged another gig, putting up signs and handing out flyers before climbing on to a makeshift stage in a vacant garage a

"They're songs about bestiality, Satanism and self-torture," Mike teased British monthly *Vox*. "We're big fans of all that crazy S&M shit. When we're not spending hundreds of dollars a week on dominatrix services, we heat up the numbers from dartboards and drop them on our skin."

couple of hours later. This was the DIY punk ethic to the core.

The band's approach to self-promotion had a personal touch, too, as Mike explains: "We used to go out and print merchandise over our guitar cases," he says. "People would bring along their own shirts, and we'd just charge them for the print. That's what kept us out on the road and sold us a lot of independent albums. That was the whole cool thing about our first two albums. No one else would tell us how to make them sound."

The band always traveled pretty light—unlike some leather-clad metal rockers, they didn't bother with a truckload of colored lights and six-foot bass cabs. Their motto has always been 'Have geetar, will travel.' Tre favors DW drums with a Noble & Cooley snare. Mike has a Gibson bass

41

and Ampeg amp and, says Tre, "Billie Joe plays out of a Marshall with a Fernandes guitar, made in Mexico... His dad bought it for him. He won't play anything else; he's got an SG and a Rickenbacker, but he hates them, doesn't play them."

On the next big U.S. tour, Tre's dad became the official driver, buying up an old library truck from Phoenix, ripping out the inside and installing bunks and equipment racks.

"Because we've been touring since we were 16, we've been to 48 of the 50 U.S. states, and gave it our all in every city, no matter if there were ten people or 500," says Tre proudly. "We've been playing around, selling our records and urging people to bootleg our stuff. We seem to do better in Chicago and Seattle than anywhere else, that's where we're most comfortable. I don't know if that translates into record sales. I don't really keep track of that sort of thing. We have a strong foundation, definitely, that's why we sell a lot of records, not because of any label."

BEERS, INSIDE AND OUT

At the end of 1991 the trio made their first tour of Europe, driving around Spain with another band and their crew—all ten men and instruments squeezed into one undersized van. In all they played 64 shows in three months, sleeping in the van or on people's floors. In Denmark, they played in a Copenhagen squat with armed guards and barbed wire to keep police out and 500 drunken fans inside. After that, they had to beg and borrow equipment every night, since the gallons of beer sprayed all over

> "I think I have a bit of an alcohol problem right now. I drink every day and I use it as a crutch to relax me. I'm not abusive, I just think I drink a little too much sometimes."
>
> *BILLIE*

them had finished off Mike's bass and a couple of amps besides. "In Denmark, if they like you, they throw beer at you," was Mike's conclusion. "So that was pretty much it. Our instruments were toast."

"Our first European tour really brought us together as a band because we were headlining shows and most people hadn't heard of us," remembers Tre. "But there'd always be a few hip people who would have our stuff, so they'd tell all their friends to come. There would be anywhere between 50 and 500 people in places like Germany, Poland and Spain. I guess in Spain right now we're pretty popular—our album [Dookie] has sold more over there than the other European countries combined. I'd prefer to tour Europe any day rather than the States."

But while playing to drunken fans Green Day remained more sober on the stage. As Billie Joe says, "I like to smoke pot when I'm trying to be as mellow as I can. I can't play in front of people stoned, because it makes me totally paranoid. If I smoke pot onstage I completely turn around and just play with Mike and Tre like we're

43

at practice—just not saying anything to anybody. I can't deal with a lot of people when I'm stoned."

Green Day have never been shy about discussing their use of drugs—over the years they developed a reputation on the East Bay scene as notorious dope smokers, a reputation which they relished. In an age where political correctness, moderation, prudence and maturity are deemed to be the keys to success, Green Day represent the extreme opposite. Their blatant and proud discussion of drug use is a flagrant stab into the heart of authority. Even the band's name is a tribute to the joys of recreational drug intake—but the liberal use of marijuana is not their only vice.

For Billie Joe, Mike and Tre, heavy drinking had always been a lively escape from boredom—whether at home or on the road. Billie Joe also saw it as an aid to his creativity, a way to help break down his self-imposed inhibitions. As an early inspiration he looked to seminal Eighties new wave band the Replacements, who championed alcohol as an essential fuel for self-expression. "They took drinking a lot to this new art form level," says Billie, "not about being a total idiot, but about being this beautifully perfect drunk. I know that when I drink it makes me able to relax and not care as much, and when I write lyrics it

"I was a speed victim until I was 18," says Billie Joe Armstrong. "I did more speed than you could possibly imagine. I never saw it as a problem, but in the end I quit because there were too many coming-down periods."

> "I like to smoke a couple of hours before the show, to get in the right mood... I get mad when people are against pot. That's what makes me mad. It should be legalized. Do it! Do it, but don't give the control to the big tobacco companies."
>
> *TRE COOL*

allows me to go at it with no holds barred and attack what's on the paper. When I'm sober, I think 'Maybe I shouldn't.' It's kind of pathetic, but..."

Likewise, drug use offered Billie Joe and the band the same gateway to creative inhibition—what Aldous Huxley described as "The Doors of Perception" following his hallucinogenic experiences with mescaline and LSD, or acid.

HEAVENLY TRIP

"For people on earth," supposes Mike, "it's probably the closest thing there is to religious heaven. I've had acid trips where I thought I was in heaven. I'm swaying there, I've left my body and my mind is just floating around. I don't have a problem in the world. And then my girlfriend walks in and that's heaven. I'm not just talking about shagging, either; just hanging out."

Mike controversially told *Rolling Stone*: "I think drinking and doing drugs are very important. When Billie gave me a shuffle beat for 'Longview,' I was flying on acid so hard. I was laying up against the wall with my bass lying on my lap. It just came to me. I said, 'Bill, check this out. Isn't this the wackiest thing you've ever heard?' Later, it took me a long time to be able to play it, but it made sense when I was on drugs. To me, everybody should drop acid at least once. Well, some people don't have the right personality for it. But it *is* important."

The most significant use for drugs on those endless tours was to maintain the band's stamina. Just as John Lennon and Paul McCartney used to pop slimming pills ("Prellys") to help them play 12-hour sessions in sweaty Hamburg nightclubs, so Green Day turned to amphetamines to sustain the buzz of performing night after night.

"The main thing of choice for us—well, Tre really likes pot—but the main thing of choice was speed," says Billie. "People think that we're this big pot-smoking band even though we sound like an amphetamine band, but I dabbled a lot in speed for a long time. That was the drug of choice on the scene I came from."

Tre, of course, disagrees: "When people bring weed to our shows, I'm the guinea pig. If somebody throws a bag of weed on stage, Billie will watch to make sure we don't get all fucked up on it, but I dive right in."

Although a fervent believer in the positive uses of drugs, Billie Joe is unsure about the effects of legalizing

"People think we're this big pot-smoking band," says Billie, "but I dabbled a lot in speed for a long time. That was the drug of choice where I came from."

marijuana. Like everything in his chaotic, unpredictable life, maybe the biggest buzz comes from the danger of it all. He confessed to cult magazine *High Times* after a trip to the free-spirited city of Amsterdam, Holland: "I really missed sneaking around someone's back to buy pot; it kind of takes the adventure out of it. It's like punk rock becoming mainstream."

ENTER THE WEASEL

After three years of hard work and good times with Lookout! records, a lot had changed for Green Day. When they weren't out on tour, Billie and Tre were sharing a basement apartment, less than a mile from the UC Berkeley campus. Their live dates were selling out and even Gilman Street was becoming too small a venue to accommodate their fans. Billie was recording new songs on his own four-track portastudio—sometimes just vocals and guitar, sometimes playing all the instruments himself.

Musically they were at a creative high—so much so that they looked beyond the confines of their own band to play and record. Billie was regularly singing and playing guitar with the Lookout! band Pinhead Gunpowder, whose album *Jump Salty* featured 12 tracks originally recorded in June 1991 and October 1992 as the *Fahizah* and *Trundle & Spring* EPs, with additional material from four compilation albums including 'Benetia By The Bay' from *A Can Of Pork*. The band featured Billie Joe on guitar and vocals, with members of Crimpshine and Monsula providing the backing. Billie Joe was uncredited for song writing, but the sound was every bit as accessible and

"The band would usually record a demo as soon as they had learned the song, and all the little subtleties would come later with the practice and performance. Their songs are simple, anyway, so the demos sound very good."

ROB CAVALLO

radio-friendly as his own work. Fave Green Day live cover version 'Big Yellow Taxi' by Joni Mitchell got the full-on treatment, and 'Beastly Bit' rewrote Van Morrison's 'Brown Eyed Girl' as a "Green-Haired Girl."

Not to be outdone by this extracurricular activity, Mike joined forces with old friend and Chicago hardcore stalwart Ben Weasel's band Screeching Weasel, adding his "bassmaster" activities to their parting shot *How To Make Enemies & Irritate People*. With a strictly speed-punk sound, Screeching Weasel recalled the greatest moments of the Ramones with flippant song titles like 'Planet Of The Apes', 'I Hate Your Guts On Sunday' and 'Johnny Are U Weird?' ending with an answer to Green Day's question: 'I Wrote Holden Caulfield.'

INTO THE BIG LEAGUE

"I watched them go from a bunch of kids to a group of musicians with a work ethic," says Tre's dad proudly. "On their first tour or two, it was more of a party than anything else. I

> **" A lot of shows on that tour had to be canceled because the crowds got too big."**
> *MIKE*

still scratch my head and say, 'How in the hell did they make it?' They used to practice in my living room here—a lot of the songs they did on *Dookie.* You hear it coming together and you don't expect people are going to go out and buy it. But when it does, you just say, 'Wow, that's so cool.'"

With success, Green Day's business and legal affairs grew more complex. The band had always handled their own bookings, tour management, accounts and

administration. But by the summer of 1993 there was simply too much for three kids to handle. At a gig in Trenton Gardens, New Jersey, they drew a crowd of 1,100 people. "That was unheard-of for us up until that point," says Dirnt. "A lot of other shows on that tour had to be canceled because the crowds got too big for the place we were supposed to be playing. So when we got back home, we started to think seriously about making some kind of change."

For help, they signed up with management team Elliot Cahn and Jeff Saltzman, who were already

Billie: "I think I have a bit of an alcohol problem right now. I drink every day and I use it as a crutch to relax me. I'm not abusive, I just think I drink a little too much sometimes."

52

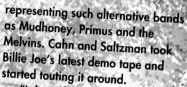

representing such alternative bands as Mudhoney, Primus and the Melvins. Cahn and Saltzman took Billie Joe's latest demo tape and started touting it around.

"I don't think they'd had anything to do with the music business," Cahn says candidly. "They were a little bit scared as to what they were going to encounter. They were cautious when they came in, but they liked the opportunities that being with a major label could give them, the money and time to make a good record, the ability to get records into stores."

By 1993, Green Day were coming to the end of a very long road and the beginning of a new, more dangerous journey. The tiny East Bay scene could no longer contain them. Next stop, the rest of the world.

1993-1994

Perhaps they should have expected it. Maybe they were naive. All they wanted to do was move on and follow their destiny, but Green Day's oldest fans betrayed them. The time had come for the band to sign a major record deal. While their friends were celebrating in their honor and wishing them good fortune in the corporate rock minefield, the hardcore punks turned nasty. Accusations of "selling out" and "breaking the code" became the bitter footnotes to Green Day's contract. But what was all the fuss about?

Music cannot be both "pop" and "alternative." By definition, the two sides are mutually exclusive. Punk music has always been fueled by the doctrine of "us vs. them." The argument goes something like this: the punks, rebels, anarchists and cooperatives produce music on their own terms for people who share their beliefs. If you don't understand them, you cannot be one of them. On the other hand, the major labels are capitalist bottom-feeders who exploit the talents of token alternative artists in order to give unearned credibility to their mainstream signings. The independent companies see the six major labels as corporate dinosaurs sucking the lifeblood from the music industry. In contrast, the major labels see the indies as a giant supermarket from which they can take their pick.

CATCH 22

As Paul Moody of Brit music magazine *New Musical Express* observed, Green Day faced the enduring Catch 22 situation of every aspiring punk band. He said that the very code of ethics of punk is diametrically opposed to the life of a pop star. He went on to pose the question facing Green Day: "whether they're willing to give up all the things that sustain them and take the leap into the unknown, cocooned

Mike on the signing war: "It was real difficult to make it through with our sanity. Major label people kiss your ass before they sign you and then they don't give a shit afterward. On Reprise it's not like that. They're for real. Everything they do, they check through us first and that makes us feel real good."

55

world where money's no problem but keeping your mental state together is."

If Green Day signed, they would not be punks any more; but if they didn't sign, they would never be anything else. Meanwhile, the major labels began to squabble among themselves, delivering new and bigger offers to Green Day's door every day.

"Warner, Geffen, Sony and everybody's mother wanted to sign us," says Tre. "But we held off for quite a long time. Why? Because David Geffen's money was paying for us to go to Disneyland. We kind of milked them. We wanted to hold out until we got complete artistic control. We wanted to be the bosses and not let somebody else tell us what to do. Of course, the first offer is bullshit, the second slightly less, the third still kind of sucks… We thought, 'Fuck this, it's our lives.' It's like getting married or something."

ENTER THE PRODUCER

By 1993, cynical major labels were already shaking off their outmoded grunge acts in search of the next alternative fashion band. When they heard Green Day's rough demo of hit-making *Dookie* material, they sprang into life. The band finally chose to sign with Rob Cavallo at Reprise Records (part of the vast Warner Brothers empire) in June.

Reprise Records' A&R (artiste and repertoire) executive Rob Cavallo made his debut as a producer in

"There are nice guys trying to be assholes and assholes trying to be nice guys," says Billie Joe Armstrong. "I'm an asshole trying to be a nice guy."

"I told Billie, 'Let's just take it as far as we can. Eventually we'll lose all the money and everything else, anyway. Let's just make sure we have one great big story at the end.' I think we will. In a lot of ways, we already do."

MIKE ON AMBITION

1993, stepping behind the boards for the first album by the Muffs, a band from Orange County, CA. While Cavallo was busy mixing the record, he received a Green Day demo tape from management team Cahn & Saltzman. Understandably impressed, he hopped on a plane to San

> "I had demos of just about everything—Billie loved to do four-tracks. He has a 16-track studio in his home, now. They were great."
>
> ROB CAVALLO

Francisco and went to visit the band in their basement apartment.

"We went out and got ice cream," he says. "We hung out for the rest of the day. We went up to the hills of Berkeley, and just kept talking, and basically I convinced them that we were the right place for them."

Cavallo was immediately Green Dazed by the three kids. "The amazing thing about them," says Cavallo, "is that they, physically and personally, were so mature. Mike plays this very progressive, very melodic bass style where there's a lot of movement. And Tre is putting in fills and he's a very adroit player—is that the right word?—he's very nimble on the drums, he puts in these fills that actually contribute to the melody. Billie is actually holding it down with a very straight rhythm. It made for a very exciting sound and I loved the lyrics and I thought their image was incredible."

Soon after that, Cavallo was asked to produce their next album. Less than three months later they

Veteran hardcore punks with a message, Bad Religion toured the world with Green Day in support to promote their *Recipe For Hate* album.

arrived at long-established Fantasy Studios in Berkeley (formerly a second home to Creedence Clearwater Revival). The band wanted to be close to home so that they could ride their bicycles to work! The album took nearly five weeks to record, working 12 hours a day from noon to midnight. Immediately afterward they set off around the world supporting veteran LA hardcore band Bad Religion's Recipe For Hate tour.

After the tour was over, some recording and all of the mixing took place in Los Angeles. They had decided to re-record the original version of 'Longview' because, while out on tour, Tre had refined and improved the song. He needed an extra large drum room to record the opening tom-toms and the track was cleverly mixed so that the rhythmic

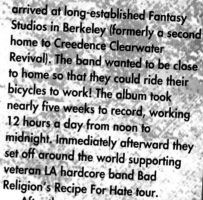

yum!

In 1994, Bad Religion joined the sell-out controversy by signing with Atlantic Records after 14 years on their own independent label. Their next album, *Stranger Than Fiction*, was widely acclaimed as one of their greatest.

drum sound would fade gradually up from the chaotic climax of 'Chump'.

ONE FOR THE MONEY

Although there were many punks who ostracized Green Day, many fans—old and new—stepped forward to offer their support. However, according to Larry Livermore, who has remained their great friend, both sides were simply missing the point. "The principal misconception is that Green Day's move was based mainly on money," he points out. "No doubt money was a factor in their decision, but, as I and others have often tried to point out, major vs. indie is not a simple equation of big money vs. little money or no money. Most bands who sign to majors never see any money except (if they get one) their initial advance. Out of the handful of bands who do make money on a major label, even fewer make any truly significant amounts. Those few, of course, become fabulously rich, just like the handful of athletes or movie stars who make it to the big time. And it's from there that most misconceptions about being on a major label arise..."

True, record contracts are signed every day, but not everyone can take their place at the top of the charts. So what makes Green Day so different? Livermore continues: "Unlike most bands who go to a major label, in the

long run Green Day will probably make a great deal of money and, at least at the rate they're going, become fabulously successful. But they're the exception to the rule, a rather large exception. And what's more they're sufficiently talented that they would have become fabulously successful even if they'd stayed on an indie label, though their success wouldn't have come so fast and might not have been quite so fabulous."

After a decade running Lookout! Records, Larry Livermore has learned what it is like to be a big fish in a pretty small pool. He knows the limits of the independent music scene and he is well acquainted with the big, wide world. There are a number of things, he admits, that Lookout! Records could never offer to a band like Green Day: "For example, we don't have the ability to get them on MTV, or on to all the commercial radio stations or into every record store in the land. Depending on your own beliefs, that might be an advantage or a drawback. But undoubtedly a large factor in Green Day's choosing the path they did was the fact that they wanted those things."

Friend and *Maximumrocknroll* columnist Ben Weasel sums up the debate: "If you sell 60,000 albums on Lookout!, you'll be set for at least a few years, assuming your needs and tastes are like those of the average Joe. If you sell 60,000 albums on [a

Jeff Saltzman and Elliott Cahn's music business clients included the Melvins, Hammerbox and Primus, along with Green Day's Reprise labelmates Mudhoney.

yum!

63

> "A lot of people, when they talk to me, I can't wait for them to shut up...Like, *shut up, you're a moron.* I have nothing to say to you, you know? I'm not trying to enhance the conversation, so shut up."
>
> *BILLIE*

major label] it's unlikely that you'll see a dime and if you're lucky, they might give you one more chance to make some real money before they drop you like a bad habit."

PSEUDO-PUNK SELL-OUTS

The band's reaction to the debate surrounding the "sell-out" was a mixture of anger and bitterness. "It came down to two groups of people," says Mike analytically. "Those who were actually worried about us, and those who never cared and just wanted

to talk shit. I'd just go up to 'em and say, 'Ya wanna talk to me about it?' and the ones who didn't care would get really aggravated and violent. Others, I could sit and talk to, and they'd eventually make sense of it all."

Bizarrely, some over-zealous punks have behaved like self-appointed crusaders, punishing Green Day for selling out. "This kid got in my face at a show," says Mike. "He wanted to fight me and I just said 'Look, man, when you actually do something for the punk scene other

65

than come to shows, get drunk and fight, and when you've played close to a thousand shows, then you can talk to me. You have no idea what it's like to be in my shoes.'"

The violent punk debate came to a head with the June 1994 issue of punk bible *Maximumrocknroll*, with a highly controversial piece slamming the corporate music industry. The front cover featured a photo of a faceless rock star shoving a pistol into his mouth with the caption: "Major Labels: Some of Your Friends Are Already This Fucked." Although the magazine and its radical editor Tim Yohannon had never been great champions of the band, many of the issue's poison darts were aimed squarely at Green Day. In short, they pronounced Green Day to be pseudo-punk sell-outs.

Billie Joe takes the subject of

punk rock very seriously. "I get really confused as far as punk rock goes," he admits. "The subculture has suddenly become really fashionable and here I am calling myself a punk. Is what I'm doing really punk rock? Staying in the Sheraton and doing a *Rolling Stone* interview? Is that necessarily punk rock? For me it's more a state of mind, but I guess on the surface it's maybe a little bit contrived. I think what I'm trying to say is that rock'n'roll is in a big identity crisis. It's not necessarily dead, but I think a lot of people don't know who they are."

However, on the subject of *Maximumrocknroll*, his opinion is clear. "Tim Yohannon can go and suck his own dick for all I care," he says. "He doesn't know what the fuck he's talking about. I've never waved a punk rock flag in my life."

"We have a lot of punk rock in our background, but I *don't* think it's something for the masses," explains Billie. "Now, we're just doing something a little bit different. We don't wanna stick ourselves in one genre for the rest of our lives. At our live shows there's been a whole new generation of people coming out and I don't have a problem with that at all. You always get nostalgic about certain things from the old days, but we're comfortable doing what we're doing right now. I mean, we had five weeks to do the new record instead of two days."

The origin of Dookie? "We personally believe that dogs are going to take over the world," jokes Mike. "And when they do, they're gonna hit everyone with shit."

67

1994

"If you can say the word 'dookie'," Mike claims, "you can keep in touch with the child within. I've always thought that's part of our success—we're immature."

Green Day's scatalogically-titled debut Reprise album was released in February 1994 to great critical acclaim, beginning a year which would utterly change their lives. It was the year that Green Day took over America. It was a year of almost constant touring across the USA and Europe as their music took a stranglehold on MTV and spread from one radio station to another. Dookie was perhaps best summed up by Simon R. Barry in cult British monthly e.p. magazine: "Third album and major label blues? Not a bit of it. Sharp, angular and angst-ridden, with all the boredom and pains of growin' up." He reckoned Dookie should be filed under "essential" along with their first two albums. "Grunge is dead, long live Green Day," he concluded. "Hell yeah, take me away to paradise."

The New Musical Express described the sound as a combination of "gonzoidpunk guitars" and "shiny happy pop tunes that really belong on another record altogether."

It's no coincidence that the lyric sheet has the words "bored," "boring" and "dead" inked in bold on

> The songs on *Dookie* were all new—a lot of them were written in the summer of 1993 while the signing war was raging.
>
> *BILLIE*

Dookie's opening track, 'Burnout'. That heavy dose of self-loathing sets the tone for this, Green Day's finest work to date. "I write better when I'm stoned," says Billie. "Like 'Burnout'. I wrote that when I was stoned on the way home from Laytonville. It was kind of like all I do is smoke pot and do nothing. I'm a fucking burnout and an idiot. I'm a fucking idiot anyway, but sometimes you feel like an idiot times ten when you're stoned."

ON THE UP

Despite the negativity of the lyrics, the whole album is unmistakably upbeat, a total adrenaline rush from beginning to end.

'Having A Blast' may be a song about killing yourself and taking the whole neighborhood with you, but it's deceptively cheerful, too. 'Chump' is the most oft-quoted Green Day song of all time, its stubborn opening gambit "I don't know you / But I think I hate you" taking political correctness back to square one in a single, infectious swipe. It was described by the *LA Times* as, "today's equivalent of the Ramones' 'Beat On The Brat'," adding that "this kind of retrogression isn't normally good in pop, but the spit in these jabs at youthful apathy and confusion is likeable and invigorating."

The singles 'Longview' and 'Basket Case' are equally shameless and profane, advocating not only masturbation but whoring, as well. The wittily-chosen words "Peel me off this velcro seat and get me moving" have been described as a "classic *Beavis And Butthead* line."

'When I Come Around' is an altogether lighter, more bouncy melody, although it's not so much a love song as a better-the-devil-you-know-song. 'Pulling Teeth' is a feverish tale of a boy who *really* suffers for love, and 'She' is a poem of despair from a life without any meaning beyond "someone else's point of view." On the positive side, 'In The End' is a song from a spurned lover who has figured out that he is better off and 'Coming Clean' is about having the courage of your own convictions, no matter how hard it might be. Billie Joe candidly explains his inspiration for the song: "Kids will always stop to think about the facts of the possibilities of not knowing what their sexuality is all about: 'Am I homosexual? Am I bisexual? Am I heterosexual? Am I no sexual? Or am I just plain sexual?' People don't know what the fuck they are. I still struggle with that, too—it's part of adolescence and growing up."

And, of course, the closing track (but for the brief, last-minute cabaret toon tacked on after a few moments of silence at the end) is the all-defining 'FOD', shorthand for that all-purpose insult, "Fuck off and die." Smutty, brash, loud and vitriolic, Green Day have not left their punk

roots behind just yet.

"Green Day is showing all the signs of becoming the next Nirvana, or damn close," comments Ben Weasel. "I'm happy for them. I wouldn't have done it their way, but it seems to be working out for them... People in the punk community don't like the fact that Green Day have attracted this huge audience with a lot of boneheads, but it's still a good album. If you liked them before, but you don't like this album, then it's for political reasons, not musical reasons."

Billie Joe Armstrong: "A lot of people, when they talk to me, I can't wait for them to shut up. Like, shut up, you're a moron. I have nothing to say to you, you know? I'm not trying to enhance the conversation, so shut up."

THE RIGHT TIME

Prompted by Reprise Records, the media began slowly to awaken to the joys of Nineties punk rock. As Green Day began their record-breaking sell-out tour, critics all across the U.S. were invited to watch the band. Most, if not all, left the venues as born-again punks, baptized in phlegm. Billie Joe's fondness for spraying gobs of greenie into the audience certainly featured in most live reviews. On a number of occasions he hauled a lunatic member of the audience up onstage to spit a souvenir ball of spittle into the fan's mouth.

High school dropouts of the nation unite at Lollapalooza—a touring summer festival featuring Green Day, L7, the Beastie Boys, Smashing Pumpkins and more.

> "It was real difficult to make it through with our sanity. Major label people kiss your ass before they sign you and then they don't give a shit afterward. On Reprise it's not like that. They're for real. Everything they do, they check through us first and that makes us feel real good."
>
> *MIKE ON THE SIGNING WAR*

Frequently, he would gob straight up into the air and catch the spit again on its way down. It was gross behavior, sure, but no less than the crowd expected from the notoriously bratty dropout. The press were grossed-out, yet strangely fascinated, growing to love the band more and more with every unique, spontaneous performance.

For their part, Green Day were as candid and amiable with journalists as with their fans. Many writers pinned their hopes on Green Day as a

Despite their success on radio, Green Day's singles have never been made commercially available in the U.S., although collectible promos are not too hard to find.

Billie on being a fan: "I remember standing right next to Kurt Cobain backstage at a Nirvana concert about two years ago. I really admired him. I just sort of sat next to him and looked at him and I was like, 'Oh fuck it.' I just walked away. I'm sure he had people hounding him all the time, so I chose not to do it."

refreshing alternative to the morose grunge metal acts from the stale Seattle scene. For instance, Steven Blush, in his *Kerrang!* magazine review of the Irving Plaza gig in New York on March 17, described the band as "pop purveyors of fun music in this new lame age of faux hard-asses and Rap Metal losers."

Manager Jeff Saltzman agrees that the band were in the right place at the right time, making the right sound:

"People were ready to embrace something new," he says. "Seattle's thing was played out, and this was, like, the next thing. We all thought it would do well, because it was great music, but I don't think anybody dared to believe that it would go to three-and-a-half-million records."

PERMANENT RECORD

On March 11, Rob Cavallo went down to Florida to record Green Day live in concert. Intended as extra tracks to appear on European B-sides, the recording turned out to be something very special to them. "I thought it was important," says Cavallo pensively. "I could see that the band was gonna be great and I could see that their show was changing as they got more mature. I thought, 'Nine months from now, this show is gonna be a different show.' I thought it was really important to document one of those early sessions before they became big stars.

"A month or so later I actually did it again in Spain. That's one of my fondest memories, going to Spain and recording with those guys. Four or five days on the road with them and it was awesome. When I got to Spain we were all excited to see each other, so we were jumpin' up and down. I met a load of people and we ended up just having one of those great times. Next thing I know I'm around a table with 16 people. We were just on top of the world because everything felt right. We went to the show that night and the Spanish punk kids were great.

"Then we got in our buses and caravanned along with another band—Los Clavos, which means The Nails, a Spanish punk band who were great kids—and for the next three or four days we would go from one city to the next and we just partied our asses off for four days straight! I didn't sleep a wink! And then, on the last day, we got to Barcelona and checked into a hotel and the 24-track recording truck turned up… and basically, we got more Green Day magic on tape."

A few days later, Cavallo and the band went on to England to record a session at the famous BBC Maida Vale

In Seattle, Green Day were supported by Hole, featuring Kurt Cobain's widow, Courtney Love, in her first major hometown appearance since the singer's suicide. The benefit gig sold out in a matter of minutes.

Studios for Radio One FM, which was later voted by the listeners as Number 2 Session of the Year.

LOSING MONEY, MAKING FANS

Although their stage shows were wild and seemingly out of control, Billie Joe and the band always kept one eye on the crowd at the front, aware that some of their new fans would not be prepared for the dangers of "moshing." Although the band have always behaved recklessly on stage—leaping off speaker stacks, pillow-fighting, stage diving and so on—Billie would frequently advise the audience to be careful. At every show he would warn the crowd to have consideration for other people or help out fans who were in danger of being trampled.

In many ways, the band was unnerved by the violence in the crowds. Mike remembers a gig in Salt Lake City where a moron was diving from a balcony on to the people below: "He jumped off twice and the second time he jumped off he knocked himself out. He was out cold. Everybody got out of the way, he hit the ground and they had to

> "We've lost thousands of dollars on this tour. Something like $15,000. Doesn't sound like a lot but I guess it is... We don't make a dime off our tee-shirts."
>
> *MIKE*

drag him outside."

The 1994 tour schedule visited Europe twice (in spring and fall) and crisscrossed the USA numerous times. To bring new faces to the shows, the band decided to keep the door prices very low, with a rule that no ticket could cost more than $20. Some gigs cost as little as five bucks! "We've lost thousands of dollars on this tour," admitted Mike. "Something like $15,000. Doesn't sound like a lot, whatever, but I guess it is... We're selling our T-shirts really cheaply and we don't make a dime off them... our merchandise guy gets really upset when people bitch about a ten dollar T-shirt. Any lower than that and we've got to pay."

On the subject of losing money, Larry Livermore sceptically points out that this kind of tour schedule would have ruined most bands. "Nearly every show sold out, a thousand or more fans at each one," he says, with pride. "And how much did Green Day make on tour? Less than nothing. In fact they lost money, a lot of it. Not because anything went wrong; in fact they expected to lose money going into it. That's the way that Warner Brothers does things: tours are seen more as a way of promoting the record. By contrast, on their last couple of independent tours, playing fewer shows and to smaller audiences, Green Day made a lot of money."

Whatever the motive, it certainly paid off. It was physically and mentally exhausting but, by the end of 1994, Green Day were on the crest of a wave. At first, sales of the album were not significantly high, but all that

Lollapalooza, Downing Stadium, Randalls Island, NY.

changed with the release of their first Reprise single,.

TAKING THE LONGVIEW

In May 1994, a song about masturbation rocketed to the top of the *Billboard* modern rock chart for two weeks, eventually notching up enough sales to rate as Number 3 modern rock single of 1994. Featuring live versions of 'Christie Road', 'FOD' and 'Going To Pascquala', the 'Longview' CD single was a perfect encapsulation of Green Day past and present.

"Green Day's first official release over here, and quite marvellous it is too," pronounced the British rock bible *New Musical Express*, reporting the arrival of 'Longview'. "A slinky bass-rolling verse, lazy and subdued, which suddenly turns into a juggernaut chorus with a deceptively acid-dipped lyric raging about slacker sloth."

The video became an instant favorite on MTV, quickly being playlisted for heavy rotation and eventually becoming Number 18 in MTV's end-of-year Top 20. The three-minute promo was filmed in the band's own apartment-cum-rehearsal space in Berkeley.

"The room that I first saw them in is the room where we made the 'Longview' video," boasts producer Rob Cavallo. "That's the basement. It's on Telegraph and Ashby, right in the heart of Berkeley. They had the basement apartment, and it was shared by Billie, Tre, Tre's girlfriend,

Billie's girlfriend at the time, a guy named Ben who was their tour guy/roadie/manager, and two other kids—one guy named Tad and another guy, I can't remember his name. They had a bunch of small rooms and one of them was the practice room—because it was underground they could get away with playing and nobody would hear them.

"A few bands would practice down there, in that space. I love seeing that video because it reminds me of what I saw when I first went down there—it's exactly what I saw. We played some guitars and got stoned—where the camera is in the video is where I was sitting when I was first there. So it's kinda great for me to see that video."

The video won the hearts of

frustrated kids the world over as Billie Joe ripped up his furniture in a dizzy guitar frenzy. The film clip went on to win two prizes at the *Billboard* Music Video Awards.

The extra pressure did no harm to the sales of *Dookie*, which spiraled uncontrollably upward. But the touring never let up. Green Day joined in the open air Lollapalooza Tour for the second month of the alternative extravaganza, replacing the Boredoms as the opening act. Lollapalooza had begun three years earlier as a U.S. version of the popular European festival circuit. The idea was to bring together an eclectic mix of music for all tastes, music to be enjoyed for its own sake, rather than just as a fashion accessory. The first bill had included such diverse artists as the Butthole Surfers, Ice-T and Living Colour.

In 1994, Green Day joined L7, A Tribe Called Quest, George Clinton, the Beastie Boys and Smashing Pumpkins in an all-day summer lineup. The band gave it their all—despite playing in the glare of the early afternoon sunshine—picking up thousands of new fans on the way. At one memorable show, as the punk sell-out debate continued to rage, girl grunge band L7 hijacked the stage in a mock protest half-way through Green Day's set, holding signs reading "Punk For Sale," "KaChing,

One of 1994's coolest rarities was a British double EP on the Fierce Panda label called *Built To Blast* featuring 'Christie Road' plus tracks from U.K. bands Fabric, Flying Medallions and Understand.

KaChing," and simply "$." Billie could hardly stifle his laughter as he tried vainly to continue singing.

THE BIG DAY

In the midst of all the madness of rapidly escalating fame, if not yet fortune, Billie Joe Armstrong got married in July 1994, to his long-time girlfriend, Adrienne.

"I was really nervous, so I started pounding beers and so did Adrienne," he said later. "The ceremony lasted five minutes. Neither of us are any religion, so we pieced together speeches. One Catholic, one Protestant, one Jewish. It was a lot of fun. Then we went to the Claremont hotel and we fucked like bunnies.

"Then, the next day, Adrienne says that she's been feeling weird lately, so we stopped at Safeway and picked up a pregnancy test. We're at home waiting for the results and each wanting the other to go check. Finally I said 'Fuck it,' and went into the other room. Sure enough, we had the big purple line. It was so bold, just staring me in the face. Purple! Baby! I walked out and said 'Hi, Mom.' I was glowing. I said 'Are you happy?' and she said 'Yeah, totally. Are you?' And I said 'Yeah, totally.' We just got married and find out the next day she was pregnant. What a high. But the thing is we'd been doing it and not using protection anyway." There was more good news on the way.

Following Green Day's now-legendary show at the gigantic Woodstock 25th anniversary show—billed as "two more days of love and music"—sales of *Dookie* finally inched past the two million mark.

> "To tell you the truth, it was the closest thing to total chaos I've ever seen in my life. The audience took over everything."
>
> BILLIE ON WOODSTOCK 94

This was surely no coincidence; Green Day's bizarre appearance on August 14 was the highlight of the weekend, the moment when the self-important, bullshit rock myth-making reputation of Woodstock was forgotten. Instead, the crowd became a crazed, mud-flinging mob, helping Green Day to bring madness to the masses. "It's completely mad," said Tre Cool later. "Like just a sea of people, a bunch of specks instead of a few faces. It's really incredible when you're playing and you look out into the crowd and you can see seven different slampits! Seven fuckin' pits, out as far as you see and everyone partying... it's like 'Wow!'"

"Going into it," Billie Joe later admitted, "I thought that the nostalgia reasons behind the show were kind of a joke. I mean, at least they could have come up with something new. So we went in thinking 'This is lame.' But then it turned into something completely different from what I'd expected. To tell you the truth, it was the closest thing to total chaos I've ever seen in my life. The audience took over everything. I saw police and guards throwing down their badges, quitting on the spot, saying 'I can't do this

any more.' Technically, it was a human disaster. Everybody was living like dogs, pretty much. If in another 25 years they have a Woodstock Part III, we're probably going to be the only band from this one that's going to be able to play it—because everybody else is going to be old or dead."

Billie Joe's mother was reportedly not too impressed by her youngest son's performance at the Woodstock fiasco. When he got back to his apartment, there was a "hate letter" waiting for him. She had seen the whole ugly thing on pay-per-view. "She said that I was disrespectful and indecent," the bug-eyed boy confessed later, "and that if my father was alive, he would be ashamed of me. She couldn't believe that I pulled my pants down and got in a fight onstage. Everything's fine now, but her letter was just unreal. She was not happy with my performance at all. She even talked shit about my wife, Adrienne, and said how she's supposed to be my loving wife, but she's never even come over and visited. It was pretty brutal."

"BASKET CASE"

Released in August, close on the heels of 'Longview', Green Day's next CD single stayed lyrically on familiar territory. 'Basket Case' had more tales of familiar territory—more tales of repression and manic depression in the Bay Area suburbs. "It's a schizophrenic thing," explains Billie Joe. "It's great to be bored, sit in a room like a complete bum—fuckin'-A! But if you don't eventually lash out against it, you become a neurotic basket case."

The new single featured some new tracks for fans desperate for more. 'On The Wagon' was the first original Green Day track to appear since *Dookie*'s release. Alongside this was a faithful tribute to the Kinks' classic 'Tired Of Waiting For You' and a new version of their own minor classic '409 In Your Coffeemaker'.

Green Day's success grew and grew. The single spent a spectacular six weeks at Number 1 in the U.S. modern rock chart in August and September 1994 and was overall Number 4 in the year-end countdown of *Billboard*'s modern rock chart.

Tre Cool sometimes appears onstage in women's clothes. Billie Joe, on the other hand, prefers to emphasize his manhood.

The video was another MTV smash hit, a surreal vignette of life in an asylum where the nurses gave narcotic candies to patients in sumo wrestler masks while the band jumped around frenetically in boiler suits and pink fish swam giddily past their faces. It was a joyous snippet of Green Day lunacy, so popular that it became MTV's Number 1 for 1994.

Britain was still slow to catch up with the band's rocketing popularity Stateside, although U.K. teen mag *Smash Hits* was sharing the excitement: "This is one to make your mum hammer on the bedroom door cos it sounds like you're smashing up your wardrobe. And the funny thing is—you will be, cos it's quite the most fantastic bedroom-trashing anthem in too long a while. Now where's that hairdye...?" However, not everyone had a kind word for the band. In its review of 'Basket Case', one stern scribe in Brit music weekly *Melody Maker* was provoked to comment: "I loathe them with every fiber of my being." Well, you can't please everyone.

THE BOSTON PARTY

Green Day brought chaos and confusion to thousands of unsuspecting Bostonians on September 9. A free concert had been arranged by WFNX, the local radio station, to take place at the city's picturesque Esplanade. A modest crowd of a few thousand happy revelers was predicted. However,

Billie on being a sex symbol: "It's weird, I mean, I consider myself kind of an ugly guy."

90

contrary to expectations, the Hatch Shell turned into a mud bath as somewhere around a hundred thousand people descended on downtown Boston. The police and state troopers were out in force, aided by a 15-man security team recruited from inmates at the local prison! Sadly, the crowd control was woefully inadequate and a few minutes after Green Day took the stage, the crash barriers came down. Then all hell broke loose.

"The police were getting beaten up and stuff," says Tre, grinning. The lighting rig started to wobble and the promoter, concerned that the whole stage might fall into the arena, pulled the plug. The crowd went mad, causing havoc which rapidly spread through the streets across the heart of the city. The local television news

Just faces in the crowd—Green Day at the MTV Awards. "You're supposed to be meeting people, but you know, I'm not going to remember any of those people," says Billie. "That's kind of sad, but it's true. Everyone's just sort of looks at you. Well, what do you want? What do you want me to do?"

reported more than 60 arrests and dozens of minor injuries from cuts and bruises. "They were tear gassing the crowd and all these things," sighs Tre, nostalgically. "Next they're announcing, 'Green Day has left the building! Green Day has left the building!' It was fuckin' funny."

In fact, the band had been ushered beneath the pavilion building for their own protection and watched the whole disastrous fiasco in

> **"This tour we've all had so many of our own problems, relationshipwise and everything, that we've all kept a lot bottled in. I'm sure every one of us, in our own way this year, has wanted to blow our fucking head off. But I think we're all not that type of personality."**
>
> *MIKE ON TAKING A BREAK*

amazement, while the prison inmates pestered them for autographs and T-shirts. "The thing is," noted the drummer, "not one of them fucked off. They all went back to jail the following day…"

The frenzied touring—as so often happens—took its toll on the band.

"Mike developed a heart problem," said Billie Joe as the end of the tour came in sight, recounting the many cruel tricks fate had played on them. "His mitral valve is too big and

sometimes it feels like someone is stabbing him in the chest. It's mostly from stress. The fact that he was born on heroin probably has something to do with it, too. Then Mike broke his teeth at Woodstock and had to have emergency oral surgery. I tore ligaments in my ankle, so I'm in a brace right now. Tre was drunk and got in a motorcycle accident in Spain. I walked into a pole and sliced open my face. Mike got in a pillow fight with his girlfriend and broke both his arms and had whiplash and six stitches in his head. Tre was drunk and fell out of a van in San Diego, Mike broke his finger ... It never ceases to amaze me. I think the only thing that could fuck our band up would be some freak accident with a vacuum cleaner."

NEARING JOURNEY'S END

As the year, and the punishing tour, approached its end, Green Day's so-called overnight success had become legendary. The huge, 16,000-seat Nassau Coliseum show on December 2 sold out in just a few minutes. With support from veteran German punks (and old tour buddies) Die Toten Hosen and comical, ultra-radical, gay punks Pansy Division, Green Day crashed down upon the Coliseum.

"Someone said to me before a show the other day, 'Fifteen thousand people at this arena—this is everything you ever dreamed of.'" says Mike Dirnt. "I turned to him and said 'Correction. It's everything I never dreamed of.'"

"Twenty years after punk rock was born, it has triumphed in ways no one expected," wrote Jon Pareles, reviewing the show in the New York Times. "He said it had survived not by conquering cities, where its speed and noise emerged, but by infiltrating the suburbs, where its supercharged message of seething boredom and aimless resentment had found receptive ears in high schools and malls. Punk had prevailed not as revolutionary music—the hope of its British wing—but because it's bratty.

"If the material's lack of diversity was obvious," commented New York

Newsday's Ira Robbins, "the songs were strong and short enough that it didn't matter. And music is only part of Green Day's equation anyway."

Playing bits of cover versions of Twisted Sister's 'We're Not Gonna Take It' and Lynyrd Skynyrd's 'Sweet Home Alabama' (sung as "Sweet Home Masturbation"), Billie Joe led the huge audience in a chant of "Fuck you!" as 15,000 wild kids flipped the bird in a wicked salute. That's the kind of audience participation that Billie Joe offers kids: "The best education they could get is coming to a concert like this," he says, seriously. "There's a time in your life where everyone's got to tell someone to fuck off. So you might as well show someone how to do it."

But Billie Joe has been known to curse his audience for treating Green Day like a stadium rock band (typical line: "Put those fucking lighters away! Who do you think we are, Bon fucking Jovi?"). The rock stadium atmosphere was noticeable among the massive Nassau audience. The fans copied every Billie Joe gesture and applauded his mock arena-rock guitar solo. They followed his cues to clap to a rhythm nowhere near the beat, but it finally disgusted him when the audience went as far as holding up flaming cigarette lighters. John

The class of 1994: With their debut, Smash, the Offspring are the first band on an independent label (Epitaph) to sell a million albums. However, Green Day are quick to deny any comparisons. "We've known them for a long time and they're nice enough guys," says Billie Joe. "But what they do is irrelevant to us."

Pareles said it all: "Punk rock is here to stay; punk independence may need a refresher course."

ONE LAST FLASH OF INSPIRATION

"Do you want to hear another one?" shouted Hole's famous vocalist, Courtney Love, to zero response from the New York crowd. "Do you want to hear Green Day?" she continued, to a riot of applause. Yup, as Ms Love put on her coat and stormed off the stage there was no doubt who this crowd had come to see. Green Day's world tour was finally coming to an end and the final date—December 5, 1994—would not pass without commemoration.

Playing Madison Square Garden is a pretty significant step in anyone's career, let alone a backstreet, know-

> "It's weird. I mean, I consider myself kind of an ugly guy."
>
> *BILLIE ON BEING A SEX SYMBOL*

nothing punk rock trio from Nowheresville, so Billie Joe honored the final few minutes of the tour in his own inimitable way: he got naked.

With the Z-100 Christmas Show (a benefit for AIDS charity LIFEbeat) beginning to drag after seven hours of Bon Jovi, Melissa Ethridge, Hole, Toad The Wet Sprocket, Weezer, Sheryl Crow, the Indigo Girls and Pansy Division, the Berkeley trio needed to be on top form to revive the flagging audience. As usual, the spit flowed bounteously, this time directed mostly at the photographers in the pit below the stage. The hits kept coming with the ubiquitous 'Basket Case', 'When I Come Around' and so on, improvizing a drag queen hoedown and playing until past 2am. In a moment of seriousness, Billie Joe reminded the audience that "One out of every ten of you will die of AIDS," but turned that frown upside down when he stepped on to the stage to perform an encore of 'She' with only a guitar to cover his shame. "His impulsive need to be noticed turned a musical endurance test into what will be one of the most talked-about concerts of the year," reported Don Aquilante in the *New York Post*. Sadly, this was well past bedtime for the band's teenage fans—who had paid $65 per ticket—many of whom had reluctantly left the building, dragged kicking and screaming to their parents' cars.

By Christmas, Billie, Tre and Mike were ready to go home. "I'm just exhausted," said Billie Joe in December, hearing a pillow distantly call his name. "Totally. We've outdone ourselves in a serious way. I have insomnia problems anyway, so it's hard for me to sleep. That's the main thing I'm looking forward to: I'll probably sleep for the rest of the year."

Twelve months of craziness were best summed up by a story that was widely reported by the press in December 1994. Apparently, in an act of inexcusable vandalism on Hollywood's world famous Walk of Fame, some deluded fan had scratched out the word "Doris" and substituted the word "Green."

The Present And Future

1995 began with the very successful release of 'When I Come Around'—a distinctly more accessible and jaunty sound for Green Day which guaranteed saturation radio play and instant chart success, topping *Billboard*'s modern rock chart for seven consecutive weeks. Meanwhile, Mike, Tre and Billie Joe had retreated to their hometown of Berkeley to get away from it all. Like Billie Joe, Tre had also married his girlfriend Lisea, who gave birth to a daughter, Ramona, in January. The couple retreated to their new home in the Oakland Hills.

Although the band members have always remained true to their fans, the past year had left them feeling drained. Tre, in particular, yearned for an end to the pressure and openly admitted that he preferred touring in Europe, where the fans were, to say the least, less fanatical. The band's sackfuls of mail left him in shock. "I go crazy when I start going through our mail," he says, reciting a typical line: "'I want to marry you, I love you, you're so cool.' *Sheeet!* No one bothers to write to us if they hate us.

We've got someone answering our mail full-time now. They have to pull out the ones they think are from our friends and stuff, or they might be getting a letter back saying 'Join The Idiot Club' or something. That's what we've got instead of a fan club—an idiot club. If you want to join it, you're an idiot, straight up! Let's see how stupid you really are—send us 20 bucks and see what you get!"

A little jaded with the adulation of teenagers, perhaps? Yearning to return to the level of his peers, to be just an 'ordinary guy' again? "You want to meet cool people and hang out with cool people," he continues,

"One day we'll either get kicked in the face, or get handed a big gold record," predicts Billie Joe, "Either way it's going to be really shocking."

101

Featuring former members of Green Day's high school rivals Operation Ivy, Rancid are now signed to Epitaph Records with a highly successful punk rock debut album, *Let's Go.*

"...but all the coolest people just fuck off right after the show because there's all these teenage idiots trying to see us. It makes us look like a big groupie band or something, and we're not at all."

AWARDS AND ADULATION

The January 26, 1995 edition of *Rolling Stone* was the annual awards issue—a very significant landmark in the world of style-conscious corporate rock. And who should be staring up from the front cover but mischievous Billie Joe, stoic Mike and just plain idiotic Tre Cool? "It's official," announced the headline inside, "Green Day are the best new band in the land. What a strange punk-rock trip it has been..."

In 1995, the plaudits came thick and fast. 'Longview' was nominated

"I'm not sure if it gets any easier as you go on," says Billie Joe, philosophically. "Look at the Beatles. Their records got sadder and sadder... The more successful they got, the more they felt they were failing, somehow."

for a Grammy award for Best Hard Rock Performance and rated by *Rolling Stone* writers as the third best single of the year. It was overall Number 3 in the *Billboard* modern rock chart for 1994. The readers of *Spin* magazine voted the single Number 5 in the end-of-year poll. Furthermore, influential Los Angeles alternative radio station KROQ named 'Longview' their Number 1 single of 1994 ('Basket Case' rated Number 8, 'Welcome To Paradise' Number 17 and 'When I Come Around' trailed behind at Number 34).

'Basket Case' was nominated for a Grammy in 1995 for Rock

"Mostly you get it from record company and merchandising people... People coming up to you and trying to bullshit with you all the time thinking that you're like *friends* or something. Its like 'No, you're not my friend. You never were my friend.' "

BILLIE .

Performance By A Duo Or Group With Vocal and readers of *Rolling Stone* voted it fifth best single and fifth best video of 1994. It was Number 4 in the *Billboard* modern rock chart for 1994.

According to *Billboard* magazine, *Dookie* was the Number 1 album for two weeks, January 29 and February 4, 1995 as it approached the end of its first year in the charts. It was 24th in the year's best-selling albums according to *Billboard*, although *Spin* magazine's own chart placed it much higher, at Number 5! The album was nominated for a 1995 Grammy award for Best Alternative Music Performance and voted the year's Number 1 by readers of *Rolling Stone* magazine in the categories: best album and best album sleeve.

The band was nominated for a Grammy for Best New Artist and swept the boards at the Bay Area Music Awards (the "Bammies") at the Warfield Theater in San Francisco, in March 1995. *Dookie* won the Outstanding Album award and Green Day were named Outstanding Group, while Mike and Tre were voted Outstanding Bassist and Drummer respectively. (The Outstanding Debut Album award went to Green Day's

"Even Kurt Cobain, with his substantial Everyman charm, was a little too fey and abstract to generate the kind of empathy with his listeners that Green Day share with theirs...

"Why else would the audience tolerate, let alone relish, Billie Joe's bantering? Essentially, they're listening to a friend talk shit."—Tim Kenneally, *High Time* magazine, January 1995.

old pals Rancid, for *Let's Go*).

Green Day were also the Number 2 Modern Rock artists of 1994, according to *Billboard*, and they were nominated for an American Music Award in the category Alternative Artist, which was won by Counting Crows.

In MTV's year-end rundown, Green Day had the Number 1 video ('Basket Case'), along with Number 18 ('Longview') and Number 70 ('When I Come Around' [Live At Woodstock 1994]). *Dookie* was voted Best Rock CD Of The Year by *Time* magazine, who said: "Do you like playing your car stereo so loud that cars in back of you flash their lights? If the answer is yes, then Green Day is for you."

Perhaps the ultimate tribute came from the novelty/experimental band

> "They're incredibly hard workers. I never got a complaint out of them— they're into getting it right. They're very focused."
>
> ROB CAVALLO

Creedle, who in the spring of 1995 released a single entitled 'It's Not Cool To Like Green Day Anymore'!

THE NEXT BIG THING

After all that acclaim and all those satisfied customers, the future looks bright for Green Day. Billie Joe's son, Joey, was born in March 1995 but his dad's break from work is due to end on June 4, when recording for the fourth Green Day album begins.

"I've heard about 14 or 15 tracks and I think this is gonna be another great record," says producer Rob Cavallo, eagerly. "I think they're very inventive. In some ways the record will be a departure, but there's some more of the same. They still have that *Dookie* music inside of them."

A few new songs have already been aired, such as the *Dookie*-esque 'Armitage Shanks', which Green Day played live at the MTV Music Awards on September 8, 1994 and 'Geek Stink Breath', which was aired on *Saturday Night Live* on December 3.

Mike on ambition: "I told Bill, 'Let's just take it as far as we can. Eventually we'll lose all the money and everything else, anyway. Let's just make sure we have one great big story at the end.' I think we will. In a lot of ways, we already do."

109

Unheard at time of going to press is another fresh track called 'Jar', which will be on the official soundtrack of *Angus*, a film about an oddball teenager and his friend. The film will also feature tracks by the Muffs, Ash, Weezer, Jawbreaker and the Dancehall Crashers. Billie has been filled with inspiration by the changing face of the band. "I've written more this past year than ever before," he says. "There's one new song about a teenage psychopath serial killer.

Billie basking in glory at the MTV Awards in 1994. "I lost the scene where I came from," he now realizes. "Not necessarily friends—I know who my friends are, who I'm going to be hanging out with for the rest of my life. I've lost the feeling of a community."

And another about kids who slack around for years waiting for their parents to keel over so they can claim their inheritance money. Kinda scary... There's also one about a girl leaving home to live in the big city, which is based on my wife."

Until the release of the next CD, scheduled for September 1995, the time will be spent readjusting to a new life, trying to integrate the punk ethic with the lifestyle of the rich and famous. Trying to be normal. "Some kids found out where Billie lived and they would hang out down the street waiting for him to come out," says Rob Cavallo. "But they're used to him now. He is kind of a local figure—he goes down to the bagel shop and people see him and there's a burrito place where people see him all the time."

"My biggest fear is becoming domestic," worries the ever-neurotic Billie. "It seems like when people get married, they don't have fun anymore. I totally want to walk around the streets with Adrienne. We like to Dumpster dive. That's the funniest thing in the world.

"I'm not going to say that I don't want to be a rock star. If you don't want to be a rock star, then quit. That's your best answer. Don't be one. But if I was to do it again, I'd do it differently. I want to try and make

> "If I was to do it again, I'd do it differently. I want to try and make some sense of all this."
>
> BILLIE

some sense of all this and not become a parody of myself. I never really thought that being obnoxious would get me to where I am right now. When I play, I'm not a nice guy. You know when you get really drunk and it's like this person inside you that wants to come out and be obnoxious? It's kind of the same thing. And then people like you for it. I don't get that."

THE END OF AN ERA

It is not only Green Day who have changed, but everyone around them. The Gilman Street scene recently attracted adverse publicity when the neo-punks turned vigilante at a show by former Dead Kennedy and political ne'er-do-well Jello Biafra. He was attacked and beaten so severely that he received a broken leg and a head

"It wasn't about people moshing in a pit and taking their shirt off. That's one thing I hate about the new mainstream thing: blatant violence."

BILLIE

injury from a mob chanting "Rock star! Rock star!"

The band are confused and disappointed by this end to an era. "I have a jaded perspective about the club," says Billie. "Hey, every good thing must come to an end."

Nevertheless, they still have the deepest respect for the club and everything it stands for, in the hope that they can remain true to that spirit

112

of cooperation. "That place was like a gathering of outcasts and freaks," says Billie Joe, nostalgically. "It wasn't about people moshing in a pit and taking their shirt off. That's one thing I hate about the new mainstream thing: blatant violence. We get lumped into this bandwagon of fucked-up mentality. To me, punk rock was about being silly, bringing a carpet to Gilman Street and rolling your friends up in it and spinning it in circles. Or having a pit with people on tricycles or Big Wheels. The whole thing had a serious message to people, but at the same time it was silly, and people weren't afraid to talk about love. It's a different thing going

"You wouldn't believe, they're not jaded at all..."—Rob Cavallo, Reprise Records, May 1995.

on there now."

Old friend Ben Weasel, now signed to the Lookout! label with his new band the Riverdales, is confident that Billie, Mike and Tre will find their way through the rock'n'roll maze unscathed. He remembers the first encounter between Screeching Weasel and Green Day with mixed emotions: "When we first met them, Mike and Billie were 17. We stayed up in the mountains at Lawrence Livermore's with them, and we were so disgusted by these guys. We thought they were the biggest idiots we ever met. They were so drunk that they were puking, and they were constantly smoking pot. So the next time I saw them I was pretty wary. They came up and they were really nice and clearheaded. In terms of how they've dealt with success, amazingly they've gotten

"Fame is a powerful drug, and I don't think it's a wholly bad one. Like any powerful drug, it needs to handled very carefully, and whether Green Day use it wisely or foolishly is up to them now."

LARRY LIVERMORE

more mature and less impressed by the whole rock star hype. They've actually become really great people."

Larry Livermore, writing his final column for *Maximumrocknroll* in June 1994, stood up for the band's integrity, as always: "Whether they're on a major or an indie, it's my opinion that with few exceptions, bands usually do their best work on their first couple of albums, and then steadily go downhill in almost direct proportion to how popular they're becoming... I think it has something to do with the way popularity and financial success isolates the band from the audience who originally gave them much of their inspiration... Fame is a powerful drug, and I don't think it's a wholly bad one. Like any powerful drug, it needs to be handled very carefully, and whether Green Day use it wisely or foolishly is up to them now."

Of course, they never much cared about the money or the fame, and they always expected to fail. They're still the same idiot clowns, dumb-ass punks playing three-chord tricks. No matter what wonders of the modern world they see, they will always be kind of bored by it all. They'll always yearn for the cracked streets and the broken homes, they'll always be whining about nothing and everything. They'll never grow up and they'll never grow old—or at least, that's what we all want to believe.

"I get mad at him sometimes because he separates himself from the family and I'm not always sure why," Billie Joe's sister Anna told *Rolling Stone*. "But he's a good boy. He's a good brother and a good uncle to my son. Success isn't going to change that. He's still the same person. I asked if there was anything he didn't want me to talk about and he said no. He said 'Tell him I pee the bed.' Because he wet his bed all through childhood. I said 'You still do,' and he said, 'I know, I just did the other night.' That's Billie Joe—he's 22 and he still wets the bed."

Discography

Sweet Children 7" EP (Skene No.10): 'Sweet Children', 'Best Thing In Town', 'Strangeland', 'My Generation'.

The Big One (Lookout!): Various Artists featuring Green Day's 'I Want To Be Alone'.

Slappy 7" EP: 'Paper Lanterns', 'Why Do You Want Him?', '409 In Your Coffeemaker', 'Knowledge' (written by Operation Ivy).

1,000 Hours 7" EP: '1,000 Hours', 'Dry Ice', 'Only Of You', 'The One I Want'.

39/Smooth: 'At The Library', 'Don't Leave Me', 'I Was There', 'Disappearing Boy', 'Green Day', 'Going To Pasalacqua', '16', 'Road To Acceptance', 'Rest', 'The Judge's Daughter'.

Kerplunk!: '2,000 Light Years Away', 'One For The Razorbacks', 'Welcome To Paradise', 'Christie Road', 'Private Ale', 'Dominated Love Slave', 'One Of My Lies', '80', 'Android', 'No One Knows', 'Who Wrote Holden Caulfield?', 'Words I Might Have Ate'.

Feb 94. *Dookie*: 'Burnout', 'Having A Blast', 'Chump', 'Longview', 'Welcome To Paradise', 'Pulling Teeth', 'Basket Case', 'She', 'Sassafras Roots', 'When I Come Around', 'Coming Clean', 'Emenius Sleepus', 'In The End', 'FOD', plus untitled bonus track.

May 94. 'Longview' CD single: 'Longview', 'Christie Road (Live Version)', 'FOD (Live Version)', 'Going To Pasalacqua (Live Version)'.

August 94. 'Basket Case' CD Single: 'Basket Case', 'On The Wagon', 'Tired Of Waiting For You', '409 In Your Coffeemaker (New Version)'.

November 28 1994. *Woodstock 1994*: Various Artists including Green Day's 'When I Come Around (Live)'.

January 95. 'When I Come Around.'

'Basket Case' (UK Import CD Single): 'Basket Case', 'Longview (Live)', 'Burnout (Live)', '2,000 Light Years Away (Live)'.

Jerky Boys OST (Atlantic/Select: 7567 - 82708 - 2): Various Artists including Green Day's '2000 Light Years Away'.

Angus OST (not yet released): Various Artists including Green Day's 'Jar'.

Chronology

1972—Billie Joe born February, Mike born May, Tre born December.

1982—Billie and Mike meet at school in Rodeo.

1985—In Mendocino, Tre is recruited into the Lookouts and given his new name.

1986—Tre plays drums on One Planet One People, the debut release on the Lookout! label.

1987—As the Sweet Children, Mike and Billie play their first gig and release their first, self-titled EP. Mike moves into Billie's house.

1989—Sweet Children are rechristened Green Day. Billie and Mike move to Oakland. They drive 200 miles to Mendocino to audition for Lookout! Records.

1990—Billie Joe quits high school. Debut album 39/Smooth is released. First U.S. tour begins the day after Mike's graduation. Drummer John Kiffmeyer leaves the band.

1991—Tre Cool joins Green Day for recording of second album. Green Day tour extensively, setting off for Europe at the end of the year.

1992—Release of Kerplunk!

1993—The band sign up with music industry legal representatives Cahn & Saltzman and are offered a contract by Reprise Records. Green Day record third album with Rob Cavallo in Berkeley and join Bad Religion on the Recipe For Hate world tour.

1994—February: Release of Dookie. Ten months of touring begins.
May: 'Longview' single is massive surprise hit on radio and MTV.
June: Maximumrocknroll magazine criticizes Green Day for "selling out."
July: Green Day join Lollapalooza tour. Billie marries long-time girlfriend Adrienne.
August: Mayhem at the Woodstock 2 festival in New York. Second Reprise single 'Basket Case' is another instant hit.
September: More mayhem when a free gig in Boston is cut short by crowd violence.
December: 16,000-seat Nassau Coliseum show sells out in minutes. Billie Joe exposes himself at a benefit gig on the last night of the tour in Madison Square Garden.

1995—Tre and his wife Lisea celebrate the birth of a daughter, Ramona, as 'When I Come Around' climbs the charts in January. Billie Joe's son, Joey, is born in March. As-yet-untitled fourth album scheduled for release in September.

117

Index

A

Armstrong, Anna 13
Armstrong, Billie Joe antics at Woodstock '94 9; background 10–14; drops out of high school 29; his son born 108; marriage to Adrienne; meets Mike Dirnt 15; moves to West Oakland 21; on drug use 43–45; on fame 111; on love 24; on selling-out 67; plays first gig 16

B

Bad Religion 59

C

Cahn, Elliot 52–53, 57
Cavallo, Rob 57–58, 77–80, 83, 109, 111
Cool, Tre background 32; gets new name 32; on drugs 47; on stardom 101–104; on the signing war 56
Corrupted Morals 22
Crummy Musicians 22

D

Dead Kennedys, The 14, 33, 112
Def Leppard 15
Dirnt, Mike background 14; joins Ben Weasel 51; meets Billie Joe Armstrong 15; moves to West Oakland with Billie Joe 21; on drug use 46–50; on self-promotion 41; on the "sell-out" controversy 63; plays first gig as Sweet Children 16
Dylan, Bob 33

G

Green Day and drug use 44–50; at Woodstock '94 8–9, 86–88; chaos in Boston 91–93; *Dookie* 68–72; first domestic tour 30; first European tour 42; first gig 22; Lollapalooza 84; Nassau 96–99; record first album 23; record *Kerplunk!* 36; sign management deal 52; signing war 56–57; the Gilman Street scene 34–35, 50, 112; the origins of the name 19–21; the "sell-out" 54, 61

K

Kiffmeyer, John 22–23, 30
Kong, Kain 33

L

Livermore, Larry 22, 32, 61–62, 81, 114
Living Colour 84
Long Ryders 24
Lookout! (label) 22, 32, 40, 50, 62
Lookouts, The (band) 32, 35
Love, Courtney 98
Lynyrd Skynyrd 96

M

Maximumrocknroll 63, 66–67, 114
Melody Maker 90
Mitchell, Joni 51
Motley Crüe 14
Mr T Experience 33

N

New Musical Express 36, 55, 68, 82
Nirvana 39, 71

O

Operation Ivy 27, 33, 35

P

Pinhead Gunpowder 50
Presley, Elvis 10

R

Rancid 34
Replacements, The 44
Reprise Records 72
Rolling Stone (magazine) 104, 106, 115
Rolling Stones, The 33

S

Salinger, JD 39
Saltzman, Jeff 52–53, 57, 77
Sobrante, Al 30
Sweet Children 16

V

Van Halen 15

W

Weasel, Ben 51, 63, 71, 114
Who, The 10, 18
Williams, Hank 10

Y

Yohannon, Tim 66–67